Cosham

The latest in our series of booklets takes us
the area on the mainland known as Cosham
the whole of Cosham but as the book evolved it became eviuent that, uu.. ..
the number of pages, this would be impossible. So in general this booklet only
covers the High Street and the streets across to Northern Road except for the
memories growing up in the area.

A second book will cover the remainder of Cosham including part of Havant
Road and the roads to the north and south.
The Highbury Estate, Wymering & Paulsgrove areas are already covered in
our earlier booklets.

Historical Background

The name Cosham has at least two origins. The hamlet belonging to Cossa
hence Cossa's Ham. Alternatively Cos refers to the broom or gorse which
grew on the hill slopes. By the time of the doomsday book it was under
control of Wymering which was a larger village and even included land on the
Island of Portsea, down to just south of Torrington Road where the former
boundary stone still stands. Later it was within two parishes, Widley &
Wymering. The new parish of Cosham was formed in December 1894 by the
amalgamation of the Widley & Wymering parishes. The village was in two
parts, East Cosham along the road to Havant, which was formerly Widley; and
Cosham on the road to Portsmouth, which was formerly Wymering.
Administratively Cosham was incorporated into Portsmouth in Nov 1920,
previously it had come under Fareham. Drayton and Farlington did not come
under Portsmouth until 1932.
Cosham High Street was part of the main road from Portsmouth leading to
Portsdown Hill and eventually onto London.
The village was principally along two main streets, High Street and Cosham
Road with houses and shops; elsewhere there were a few villas in their own
grounds. The majority of the housing on the eastern hill slopes down to the
railway were built from the 1920s/1930s.

In 1927, 22 plots on the west side of the High Street; 9 on the new North
Road; 8 on the north side of the Spur Road, 9 on the south side of the new
Spur Road were to be auctioned. They were part of the Portsdown Estate that
had been purchased by the corporation from the Thistlethwayte family, 3 plots
on the north side of Spur Road were later retained for the new Cosham
Library.

Saturday Morning Picture Club

"When I was a child, a treat for Saturday mornings was to go along to the cinema. Most of the larger cinema chains operated these clubs. It was a cinema for children only. Prices were sixpence downstairs in the stalls and ninepence upstairs in the circle. You did not need to join the club, but if you did you had a treat on your birthday, in that you had a free ticket which entitled you to go upstairs with a guest. Another way of going upstairs was to arrive a bit late and if the stalls were full you could go to the circle (you were never turned away).

The films consisted of older action films and cartoons with a serial which went on for weeks. Most of the films were made in the forties and fifties with the occasional nineteen thirties film. There was a break in the middle of the morning when the manager would come on stage invite certain children up and there would be a competition of some sort and prizes given for some skill or other. One particular time it was Yo-Yo's and another time was the use of Hoola-Hoops when these were in fashion. During the interval was also sung the club song:

"We come along on Saturday morning
Greeting everybody with a smile......"

With the demise of the cinema in the late twentieth century so ended the Saturday Morning Picture Club."

Growing up in the area

"Born in Southsea in 1943, I moved at the age of 5 with my Mother and new Stepfather to 33 Totland Road on the Isle of Wight Estate in Cosham. Amongst my earliest memories is of being unable to find my way home from my new school, Medina Infants at the top end of Brighstone Road, literally two roads away.

As I recall, number 33, a mid terraced house was very small, but I was fortunate, being the eldest sibling in having my own bedroom, very handy when sent up the 'wooden hill' on those bright summer evenings and expected to sleep .... fat chance, instead I would try and communicate with Archie Kimber across the road with our 'Tommy Walls' Morse code cards, of course with the keen eyesight of a seven year old it was quite feasible to see each others attempt to send messages, quite another to send or receive a coherent message and in hindsight it would have been easier to shout to each other, but of course that wouldn't be as cool as imagining we were secret agents and it beat going to sleep in broad daylight!

As people of my generation know, side roads were mostly free of motorised traffic as few could even think of buying a car. Totland Road, like much of the

IOW estate was, apart from the occasional bread or coal lorry, a safe play area for us local kids, so safe in fact that our mothers were often out with a skipping rope across the road with dozens of us trying to skip together. You would be hard pressed to try that today. Mind you this didn't apply to Medina Road, which although hard to believe was part of the main south coast trunk road prior to the new link road, Southampton Road, being built. Mostly there was one motorcycle and sidecar and one car parked in the whole road, the motorbike or to be more specific its speedometer always held our gang of boys interest as we were convinced that the 130 MPH shown on the dial was achievable. As this machine was well past its sell by date, probably 30 MPH was its limit! As for the solitary car it usually belonged to someone else and was being repaired by our next door neighbour who apparently was a former RAF engineer. In fact this was the first occasion I can recall of anyone doing home repairs on a car.

Our playground extended down Gurnard Road to the council play park which was near the original prefab site. Now long gone and occupied by Arthur Dann Court, a residential home. It is nice to see that the old play park was replaced by a new albeit 'health & safety' model (not nearly adventurous as my childhood memory of the old one). From here we would often run under the small railway bridge, a good place for us boys to ambush each other and have a scrap, which took us into King George playing field and to the shore beyond. The shore then was on the southern side of the now dual carriageway we know as the Western Road prior to the reclamation of the land for the former IBM site. Endless hours were spent as we recreated our version of fighting 'Jerry', which often ended up with quite a few bumps and bruises, but it could have been far worse with 'Dutch Arrows' flying around, catapults and even air pistols ... health and safety no! Happy and adventurous days, without a doubt.

Besides all this play and the distraction of TV being in its infancy, I joined the St Johns Ambulance Brigade, the cubs and subsequently the scouts which were the 24th Portsmouth Air Scouts at the long demolished Cottage Homes opposite QA hospital. Some boys residing there were members of our troop and over time following annual camping trips to the Meon Valley, Church Parades and for a lucky few flights in a RAF Chipmunk training aircraft from Hamble; plus if our parents could afford it a week long gliding course camp at Lasham Airfield. I was one of those fortunate ones and as I realised later, although my family were very much ordinary working class, I was almost privileged in comparison with some of the kids from the home and this, despite leading a normal manual working life myself is something that has stayed with me though my life.

Cosham

I then moved from the safe and calm atmosphere of Medina School to the real world, Portsdown Secondary Modern School for Boys. It has a tough reputation which was completely justified, the use of the cane was almost routine and fights, of which there were many, often led to the perpetrators being escorted to the makeshift boxing ring in the gym, fitted with gloves and encouraged to sort their differences out. However, there were some good teachers, many of whom, had served in the recent conflict of WWII so knew how to instil discipline and it wasn't until later in life that you appreciate some of their efforts and it goes without saying we could do with some of that discipline in schools today. The Boys' School has also now gone and a big regret of mine is that I didn't revisit it before the wrecking ball went in, after all whatever we went on to do in life, successful or not, school had a huge influence in shaping our character.

Through these school years and like many of my peers I joined the world of work, a daily paper round for, I believe Reads newsagent at the top of Cosham High Street, now also gone prior to the redevelopment of that area, I well remember my first day when my Dad woke me at some ungodly hour with a wet flannel on my face. However, I got through the first few days on what was my 'starter round' with a false sense of security, as when Sunday came (this was a seven day week!) I was given a satchel of enormous Sunday papers which my skinny frame could barely carry. If I thought that was bad, a few months later my round was increased with the completion of the Link Road and the newly built flats which were fast being occupied and although only three or four floors high, increased my workload enormously. Phew! The upside of my round was that the very last delivery (with comics Eagle/Beano/Dandy etc. plus the occasional 'lost' comic) was to my own house and of course I was earning some money.

Saturday morning 'flicks' at the Odeon will be remembered by most kids of the 50s and 60s, 9d from Mum for the cheap seats, stalls, where we would be inevitably bombarded with anything to hand from the 'rich kids' in the balcony, who were able to pay a bob or more, this often created mayhem with cat calls and negotiations for a scrap, despite the efforts of the despairing usherettes trying in vain to restore order, but this was soon forgotten as soon as the entertainment began, normally with a lusty rendition of 'I Love to go a wandering' following the words with the bouncy ball on the screen accompanied by the mighty organ, this was followed by a few trailers etc. for up and coming films and finally the main films when we would scream our support for the 'goodies', usually a cowboy in a white hat! Or hiss and boo at the 'baddies' who inevitably wore a black hat and looked mean. The film was often a serial and usually ended with us all frustrated to know what happened next, of course it was a clever ploy to make sure we pestered our long suffering parents for another couple of bob the following week, it also created mayhem particularly to the Saturday shoppers in the High Street as we exited the cinema ... a morning of great fun and excitement and all for 9d, although sometimes I was lucky enough to get an extra tanner to spend in the little sweet shop opposite the cinema, another casualty of the wrecking ball under I believe controversial circumstances as I think it was a listed building.

There was also a coal yard behind the picture house (Gregorys perhaps) where along with many others I was sent along with my sister's buggy to get a half hundred weight bag, most people had coal fires then, central heating, at least in my world was never heard of ... it seems an awful lot went on around the cinema, which is now a Bingo Hall, but at least it is still standing.

Time doesn't stand still and inevitably things change and not all for the better, apart from the aforementioned also gone are The George and Dragon pub where I took my wife of forty nine years on our first date, The Ship Pub, The Railway later to become The Rocket, Palm Court (Teddy Boy hangout), Woolworth, Beaumonts, Dewhurst butchers, The Co-Op, Pinks, Wilkins bakers and many others that I can't remember. We had a fully functioning Police Station which we could actually enter. Sadly though the station house is still in situ, it may as well be empty, as we the public are concerned, as with all the cutbacks today it is no longer people friendly!

On a positive note Mays Fish & Chip Shop is still serving and has helped sustain me since I first went in there as a cub for threepenneth of scraps!"

Martin Longhurst

"Of the shops I remember Christopher's shoe shop is the only one left, same door, six steps and a lift up latch. There was, by The Swan public house, Bakers Chemist that had two big medical bottles in the window with coloured liquid in them and also had a lift up latch and a high step. The others were Curtis's that sold hay, Empire Stores that was further down the High Street and Shipps. Also Threadinghams, a dark old shop, that sold a wide variety of herbs. Where Tescos now is there was a school. Next door to the Odeon there was a shop, called Davidsons, that sold hats, coats and dresses. My husband, as a boy, used to work in a vegetable shop called Smeeds at the bottom end of the street. It was a shop where all the fruit and vegetables were out on the pavement on tables. At the other end was a wet fish shop called Arnetts and he used to wash the slab down making the pavement all wet and icy in the winter."

Eve Patten

Cosham

Street List
The listing following is based on the 1960 Kellys Directory, with dates expanded where business stayed, or the trade stayed. Note where the date stops at 1976 this is only because that is the last year the directory was published and unless someone can remember we are unable to say when businesses closed or were sold. Residential properties are not included except where the house is of note or there were famous residents. The choice of 1960 means that our senior citizens will be able to reflect on their youth in Cosham, younger readers can see what was in the streets in 'olden' days, hopefully both groups will find something of interest within the booklet.

High Street
In 1930 it was proposed to widen the street from the Railway Hotel, 119, to number 13; and prior to 1940 some premises were not numbered. The street has since had more changes as larger premises were demolished and replaced and at the northern end both sides have been redeveloped.
East Side of High Street
Railway Station
>"The railway station was the hub of my social and working life because I had free transport to Fratton when I worked for British Rail. The railway station was opened in 1848. The foundation brick was laid by Mr Littlejohns of Drayton. The footbridge was built by Joseph Westwood, engineers of London, in 1890 as shown by a plaque.
>On the way to work one day I was told don't look down at the track. Others of my friends had seen what had happened, a women had thrown herself from the bridge and under a train, the whole experience really upset the ones who had seen the whole incident.
>When we travelled to work both sides of the station had waiting rooms and gas lighting was still in place. We would also see and speak to people getting off at Hilsea Halt who worked at the various factories there. My friend Patsy Vincent would point out people she knew from Highbury like ex-government men and an old gent who worked at the Guildhall. She arrived one hour early one day as she had forgotten that the clocks had gone back.
>A lot of time we worked overtime, but on regular evenings we would go up the High Street stopping at the chemist to try on new perfumes and generally look around, then we would take the turning by the health centre and telephone exchange and say goodbye and shake hands with the few people who lived on the Isle of Wight estate."
>Sylvia Webb

From here to Knowsley Road the properties have all been demolished.
Railway Cottages 1-6; 1896 to1976. They were still there in 1981.
There were also some kiosks for Colyer & Co.; W.H Smith & Sons
Ltd, Booksellers, 1908 to 1967; Pickfords, Removal, Storage & Travel
Services, 1940 to 1960.

123   Hampshire Driving Academy; Motor School; 1958 to 1967. Earlier
Rentaset; 1951 to 1956 (see 105b)

121   Clements Bros (Portsmouth) Ltd; Coal Merchants; 1934 to 1975.
Earlier Clements Bros; 1928.

The most southerly property is now Wynnstay House, at 121, with the job
centre on the ground floor, with flats above, for which planning permission
was granted in 1990.

119   Listed as the Railway Hotel or Railway Tavern in the trade directories
from 1875 to 1962. By 1964 it had become The Rocket which it
remained until it was closed. The site is now occupied by 20 flats,
Railway House, for which planning permission was given in 2012.
The flats are listed in Knowsley Road. PMC have offices on the
ground floor. (See 80)

here is Knowsley Road

117   Mrs Harriet Davis; Provision Merchant; 1936 to 1960.
Earlier H.M Davis; Provision Merchant; 1934.
Later G.S Shipp & Sons Ltd; Fruiterers; 1962 to 1976.
Now The Arts Academy, Haberdashery & Craft Shop also providing
workshops and parties.

115   A.G Mills & Co. Ltd.; Booksellers, Wholesale & Retail Stationers &
Fancy Goods; 1940 to 1966.
Later John Garland Ltd; Stationers; 1967 to 1976.
Now Taste of China, Restaurant & Takeaway, planning permission for
which was granted in 1992.

113   Carlisle's; Florist; 1940 to 1967.
Later Joan Kail; Florist; 1971 to 1976.
Now XoXo Beauty Parlour, here since May 2011 run by Twee
Nguyen and Idy Ho.

111   William Podgur; Jeweller, Watch & Clock Maker; 1938 to 1967.
Earlier Joseph Podgur; Jeweller; 1934 to 1937.
Later A Good & Son; Jewellers; 1971.
Now Tom & Holly Nail Studio.

109   Was a Snack bar for many years:

Earlier Jiffy Pies (L.F Crease) 1938 to 1951.
Mrs Mary Symonds; 1953 to 1958.
J.G Symonds;1960 to 1967.
D.G Thomas; Snack Bar; 1971.
The Jiffye Café; 1973 to 1976.
Now the Golden City, Chinese Takeaway.

107   Portsea Island Mutual Co-operative Society Ltd; Boot Dealers; 1951 to 1976.
Now Help 4 Special Children, Charity Shop.

105b   Rentaset Ltd; Radio Hire Service & Portsmouth Radio Relay Service; 1958 to 1966. Radio Rentals; Television Rentals; 1967 to 1976.
Now Pizza Hut.

105a   Was a jewellers for many years:
Hollander's; 1958 to 1962.
Bentons; 1966 to 1976.
Was later CTN Stores, papers, confectionary etc. but seems to be closed.

103-105   C.J Beaumont Ltd; Outfitters; 1951 to 1976.
"A favourite shop for the young teenager. Duffel coats, Tommy Steel sweaters and very flashy shirts"
Malcolm Garlick

Earlier the shop was Alders.
"My grandmother, Ethel Alder, then Stevens, lived here in 1947. She had a lingerie and corset shop. My mother worked for her and had to work hard from 8am til 10pm, personal customer service and all the goods in drawers. Ladies would come in and have special treatment, sat on wooden chairs while mum served them. My mother won an award for best dressed window with a child in a high chair advertising Kayso Aprons. After that as my grandmother got older she moved to Cornerways, Court Lane a large corner bungalow that was built in 1958. It had sunshades over every window and a large garden. She had posh furniture and dinner was served in silver entree dishes."
Sue Simmons

In 1961 a planning application for change of use of The Bungalow, to shop was raised. There is a low building visible over the parapet of 103-105a which could be the old bungalow that was incorporated into the shops.

In 1984 a planning application was raised for 103-105 to be used as an Amusement & Leisure Centre. Now Kingston Leisure.

here is Cosham Park Avenue
101   John Sutton-Jarvis; Chemist; 1946 to 1975.
        Now Cabella, Hair & Beauty, opened by Leigh & Lauren in 2015.
101a   Neatwear (Separates) Ltd; Ladies' wear; 1960 to 1967.
        Later Joanne Separates; Ladies' Outfitters; 1971 to 1976.
        Now Shoefix in Cosham, since 1994, shoe repairs, key cutting, engraving etc.
101b   Oanda Fashion Shoes; 1960 to 1975. The proprietors were O Birch and A Birch, hence O and A. The old signage was visible in 2017 when the premises were empty awaiting a new shop owner.

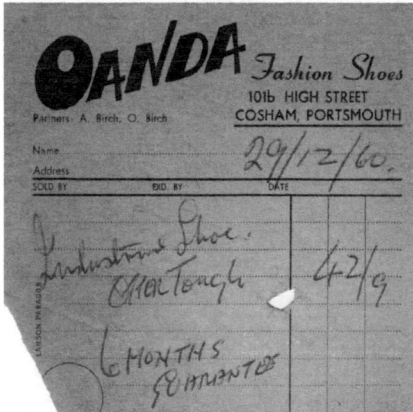

Changed from a retail shop to King & King Estate Agents in 1974. Later Mann Countrywide estate agents, now empty.
101c   Doctors Surgery for many years:
        David Rossiter & Kenneth Davies; Physicians & Surgeons; 1960.
        Later just Kenneth Davies 1962 to 1964: Kenneth Davies & Richard Green 1966 to 1967: Kenneth Davies, Richard Green, F Partington and Diana Heptinstall 1971.
99   1960 not listed.
        Later A.G Terry; Corn Merchant; 1962 to 1967: D Combes; Pet Stores; 1971 to 1976: Cosham Pet Centre in 1994.
        Now The Castle Sweets.
97   Vinson, Epps & Co.; Drapers; 1934 to 1960.

Now Headlines, Turkish Hairdressers, claims to be the only Turkish barbers in the Portsmouth area.

95   Smeeds Ltd; Wine & Spirit Merchants; 1953 to 1967.
Earlier Smeed & Smeed; 1936 to 1951.
Later The Wine Traders 1971 to 1976.
Now Lee Fletcher Funeral Services. Established in 2002.

93   J Mansfield; Confectioners; 1960 to 1966.
Confectioners for many years:
Earlier George Juster; 1934 to 1938: Mrs Juster; 1940 to 1946: Hoars; Tobacconists etc.; 1948 to 1951: Kay Davies; 1953 to 1958. Not listed from 1960 to 1966. Then Kay Davies again; 1967 to 1973: J.G Bevis & Sons Ltd; 1975 to 1976.
In 2008 a planning application was raised for use as dental surgery.
Now Cosham Dental Practice.

91   Harold Threadingham; Grocer; 1928 to 1962.
"They had an old three wheeled delivery van."
Malcolm Garlick

Later Shirt King; Outfitters; 1971 to 1976.
Now Beautiful Nail Studio.

89   The Modern Library (William Trivess); 1938 to 1962.
Earlier The Modern Library (H Knighton); 1936 to 1937.
Still there in 1964 but no mention of William.
"Many of the books had the Boots Logo from when Boots ran a lending library."
Malcolm Garlick

Now Portsmouth Ink, Tattoo & Piercing, Dermal Implants.

87   Freeman, Hardy & Willis Ltd; Boot Makers; 1937 to 1976.
Now Widley Express Convenience Stores.

85   J Baker & Co. Ltd; outfitters; 1956 to 1967. The house was converted into a shop in 1927.
"More expensive and up-market than Beaumonts. The styles suited older and more fashion conscious teenagers as well as adults."
Malcolm Garlick

Later Co-operative; Dry Cleaners; 1971 to 1976.
Now empty.

83   Midland Bank Ltd; 1936 to 1976.
Now HSBC which is due to close soon.

81   Not listed.
     Later J Baker & Co. Ltd; Outfitters; 1971 to 1976.
     Now Santander Bank, formerly Abbey (National) Building Society.
77-79 W Pink & Sons Ltd; Grocers; 1938 to 1975.
     Pinks were earlier at 45; 1928 to 1937 and 53; 1910 to 1937.
     "The cold meats used to be displayed on white pedestals."

     A planning application was raised for rebuilding in 1965 as a shop and
     flats.
     Later Moores Stores Ltd; Grocers; 1976.
     More recently Coopers Discount Shop, now Wessex Cancer Trust,
     Charity Shop.
75   Hoars; Tobacconist & Confectioners, 1948 to 1964.
     Earlier Frank Pearce; 1937: Robert Pearce; 1938: Mrs E.M Hoar; 1940
     to 1946.
     Later J.G Bevis & Sons Ltd; 1966 to 1967.
     Then became a bakers, Modern Home Bake; 1973 to 1976.
     Now Heidi's Swiss Patisserie. They have been here since at least
     1994. A local company formed in 1969, based on Hayling Island, run
     by Heidi, the daughter of Ernst Strassman who was born in
     Switzerland in 1935. He came to England after qualifying; working at
     Fortnum & Mason before starting his own business.

69-73 F Worley & Sons Ltd; Boot & Shoe Dealers; 1958 to 1971.
     Earlier at 73 only; 1951 to 1956.
     The shopfront at 71 High Street was put in by John Croad for A & E
     Chapman in 1929.
     Later National Westminster Bank;1971 to 2017.
67   J Loat; Ophthalmic Optician; 1936 to 1967.
     Earlier Montague Gluning; Optician; 1934.
     Later B.N Bungey; Ophthalmic optician; 1971 to 1976.
     Now The Goldman, since at least 1994.
65   Now Round in Circles, Fashion & Beauty.
63   A Christopher & Son; Boot Dealers; 1911 to 1976. Earlier Arthur
     Christopher, Boot Maker, 1910.
     Still there in 2017 and at Portsmouth with a branch in Kingston Road
     which opened in 1977.
     In the 1911 census Arthur, 29, Bootmaker, is shown as a lodger at
     Havant Road, with his wife Gertrude, 23 and son Arthur William, 9
     months; his birthplace was Poole.

The oldest family business in the street and probably area. Mays, Fish & Chip shop runs a close second but is no longer in the family.
"Always the place for 'ordinary footwear."
"After searching every other shoe shop in Portsmouth I took my wife to Christophers and straightaway she found a pair she liked. I always go there first."

Christophers Shop on the corner of the High Street and Magdala Road

here is Magdala Road
61   Seals of Southsea Ltd; Motor & Cycle Specialists; 1940 to 1964, at first just cycles.
F.M Seal of Highland Road, Southsea had the shopfront added in 1933.
Earlier Seals, Cycle Dealers; 1934 to 1938.
"Dad bought my first 'brand new' adult push bike there, a Raleigh Elizabethan Tourer to celebrate the coronation in 1953. Later they sold motor scooters; NSU, Primas & Lambrettas come to mind"
            Malcolm Garlick

In 2008 a planning application was raised for rebuilding as shop and flats.

Cosham

Until very recently was Quids In, discount shop. Opened in April 2013.

59a G.W Green Ltd; Bakers; 1956 to 1976.
Now Cosham Express Convenience Store.

59 Arthur May; Fried Fish Shop; 1948 to 1976.
Earlier John May; 1928 to 1946.
Still has the facia Mays and was by R.C Capaldi, but the blind says Pat & Ian's Fish Bar; and the illuminated sign says A.W May.
"The inside of the shop was tiled and I would go there to buy fish for my grandmother."
Sue Simmons

"A good chippy, the owners were friendly with my fiancé's father. They made our wedding cake."
Malcolm Garlick

57 Peters; Fruiterers; 1960 to 1964.
Earlier Lionel Horsey; Greengrocer; 1951: Ronald Horsey; Greengrocer; 1953 to 1958.
Later D Gorringe Ltd; Fruiterer; 1966 to 1976.
Then a branch of Supa Snaps since at least 1994. The shop is currently Max Spielmann - The Photo Expert. Supa Snaps started as a subsidiary of Dixons, it was bought by Sketchleys in 1993. Later with Sketchleys became part of the Mr Minit chain before closing and being sold again.

55 M Gaiman & Sons Ltd; Grocers; 1960 to 1964.
Earlier Mrs Mary Boxall; Grocer; 1934: M Gaiman; 1936 to 1958.
Later M Gaiman; Antique Dealer; 1966 to 1967.
"Gaiman's the grocery store was famous in our family for its broken biscuits."
Sylvia Webb

Was later Cosham Car Accessories from 1971 to 2014.
Established in 1968 by Bill Hensby. Closed at the end of February 2015 when Bill retired, aged 70, due to high rent and rates and drop in custom as people at present are not working on their cars.
The shop is now Cakes O'Licious, Speciality Cakes.
here is The Droke

A narrow alleyway leading to Park Lane, originally just a rough lane but now surfaced. The source of the name is not known although some say that alleys in this area were known as Drokes, however, this the only one.

"On the south side of the Droke at the back of Seals (later Cosham Car Accessories) old premises was 'Nobby' Clark a motorcycle repair man. Good at his job and a nice person in the 1960s."
Malcolm Garlick

"There was a motorcycle repair garage there, where I took my BSA to for repair. Behind the workshop the Droke narrowed down to a footpath. We used to go that way to Goodwyn's Youth Club behind the Salisbury Inn. I remember running through the Droke singing Beatle's tunes."
Frank Thompson

53   Chapman's Laundry (Receiving Office); 1960 to 1976. They had a new shopfront in 1951.
Earlier Silver Arrow Cleaners (E Chapman Ltd) & Chapman's Laundry; 1946 to 1958 at 53/53a. Earlier Chapmans were at 71; 1911 to 1940.
Now Tan & Envy.
53a   Brighter Homes, Wallpaper Merchants; 1962 to 1975.
53b   Sladen, Duff & Read, Physicians & Surgeons; 1958 to 1971.
See also 49.
Earlier Bell, Doyle & Sladen; 1937 to 1946: Doyle, Sladen & Duff; 1951 to 1953: Sladen & Duff; 1956.
"There was a long passageway with a step down at the end into the doctor's waiting room."
Malcolm Garlick

Now Thomsons, Holidays
51   Denis Naylor; Dispensing Optician; 1946 to 1976.
Number 51 was split into two shops in 1944. 51 was Access, Keys & Locks in 2014 but they have relocated to larger premises at Purbrook.
51a   Franks, Jeweller, established 1950, 1964 to 2017.
49   Was earlier the King & Queen, licensed premises, from 1847 to 1920 in the trade directories.
By 1929 was the surgery of Doctors Bell & Doyle until 1938 when new premises were built. Listed as Bell & Doyle; 1928: Bell, Doyle & Sladen; 1934 to 1936.

Later rebuilt and used by Victor Value & Co. Ltd; Grocers; 1960 to 1964.
Then Jack Grant Racing Ltd; Turf Commission Agents 1967 to 1976.
In 1998 there was a planning application for an Amusement Centre. For some years later it was Edwards Amusements, a Windsor based company who run amusement arcades and amusement parks around the country. Now Every Cloud, Vape Shop.

47   Weston Hart Ltd; Radio Engineers; 1946 to 1976.
"Many an hour was spent in the booths listening to the latest hit records. Only one was officially allowed but our gang knew the girl behind the counter, Shirley, so she bent the rules for us."
Malcolm Garlick

Younger readers may need this explaining - you used to be able to go to the music shop and ask to hear your selection before deciding to buy it - there would be a row of booths with speakers fed from equipment behind the counter. No downloading from the internet back then!

Earlier the premises was William Dashwood; Undertaker in 1928.
Now Co-op Funeral Care, so reverting back to the original use.

here is Albert Road

37-45   Have been rebuilt, planning application 1981.
45   Boots The Chemist; 1940 to 1967.
Now Costa, Coffee Shop
41-43   Portsea Island Mutual Co-operative Society Ltd; Grocers; 1918 to 1962. Later expanded into 37-43, 1964 to 1976.
"This was my first job after leaving school in 1962. I worked mainly in the food shop but also in the bread shop next door. There was a Co-op ladies' hairdresser over the bread shop.
My manager was a nice man by the name of Mr Earl. The rest of the staff were also nice to work with. My uniform was a yellow nylon overall. If I had to work on the meat or cheese counter a totally useless hair cover was mandatory. It consisted of a close fitting band with a hairnet but it was continually coming off.
My job was shelf stacking and serving behind the till. All of the goods were priced with a Chinagraph pencil and were constantly changing. Sticky labels came later. At the end of the day the takings would be given to two girls at a desk for checking.

The meat, mainly bacon, came in large pieces and had to be cut on the premises. The cheese counter had an excellent selection with reserves kept in the cellar. Cheese came in large pieces and had to be cut with a wire. I became very good at judging the required weight.

Storerooms were both upstairs and downstairs along with a staff room on the top floor. Deliveries were brought by lorry into the yard at the back and through large doors and put onto a conveyor system to be taken upstairs for storage.

We had a system whereby people could pre-order. This was done by filling in their order book and their goods were selected, placed in a box and delivered to their home. Some customers would be unable to get to the shop so I would walk to their homes, as far as Drayton, where they would give me their order. I would then walk back to the shop and their order would be attended to. All deliveries were by van. I stayed there happily for about three years but moved on to a better paid job."

       Yvonne Garlick

	Now Poundland.
39	H.F Wilton & Son; Fruiterers; 1951 to 1962. Earlier Miss C.M Fullick; Fruiterer; 1923 to 1928: Harry Frederick Wilton; Fruiterer; 1934 to 1948.
37	George Burges; Fishmonger; 1920 to 1962. Now Subway, Sandwich Bar.
33-35	Lloyds Bank Ltd; 1923 to 1976. Earlier Capital & Counties Bank; 1899 to 1918 at 33. In 1918 Lloyds took over Capital & Counties. The premises were rebuilt in 1927. A planning application was raised for change of use bank to retail premises in 1979, from 2014 to 2016, was empty although there are now signs of work at the property in 2017.
31	F.W Woolworth & Co., Stores; 1936 to 1976. Now Poundstretcher.
29	Not listed in 1960. Earlier Cosham Picture House Ltd; 1923 to 1934, Waverley Cinema. In October 1934 Mr F.W Olding, of 2 Upper Arundel Street applied for a licence to re-open the Cinema of the Cosham Picture House under the name Waverley Cinema, seating 545. It was listed under his name from 1936 to 1938. The Waverley was very narrow with five seats either side of a central gangway.

"My most vivid memory is going to Saturday morning cinema to see Flash Gordon etc for 3d. Next to the 'bug hutch' as we called it was the remains of the livestock market with the pens and rails, behind the George & Dragon pub."
Arthur Collins

The site was later used as Cosham Fire Station; 1939 to 1953.

27 Listed in the trade directories from 1847 to 1956 as the George, or George & Dragon. It was rebuilt in 1887.

At the rear was Cosham Steam Brewery, listed from 1875 it was one of the group that merged in 1896 to form Portsmouth United Breweries, when the brewery was sold for £2,500 and Whicher & Co. continued brewing on the site for some years. In 1936 a weekly market was planned to be held for eggs, live & dressed poultry, Game, Butter, Farm & Garden Produce together with 'Dead' Stock.

The George & Dragon and Woolworth in 1987

"A favourite haunt of older yokels. I was called in by Whitbreads to sort out an unspecified plumbing problem. This turned out to be rigging up a separate tap in the old yard out at the back to give a water supply for Mr Gregory's horse. This gentleman was well known in Cosham for delivering greengroceries by horse & cart. This was around 1975."

Malcolm Garlick

The George & Dragon outbuildings at rear in 1987

27a Now Ushers, Greengrocers.

27 Co-op Travel Agents.

25   Hewett Bros (Pawnbrokers) Ltd; 1938 to 1976.

Earlier George Boxall; Grocer; 1881 to 1928: Hewett Bros; Jewellers; 1934 to 1937.

25a now Clintons Cards

27 now Superdrug.

Odeon Buildings; 1948 to 1976.

Earlier Ambassador Buildings; 1937 to 1946. Now 15 High Street - Crown Buildings.

Before the Ambassador was built this was the site of the cattle market.

4a   Now Pot of Gold Amusements.

4   Finlay & Co. Ltd.; Tobacconists; 1960 to 1966.

Earlier Collis & Co. (Tobacco) Ltd.; 1937 to 1946: Hodges Easton (Tobacconists) Ltd.; 1948 to 1958.

Later Pergo Driving School; 1971 to 1973. Standen School of Motoring; 1975 to 1976.

Now L.A Barbers.

3   H Finlay; Costumier; 1951 to 1960.

Cosham

Earlier Delores; Costumiers; 1937: Seymour Fashions Ltd.;
Ladies' Outfitters; 1946: Davidsons; Gowns & Fashions;
1948.
Later 1962 to 1976 Davidsons; Ladies' Outfitters.

Joe Davidson who ran the ladies wear shop was once Lord Mayor of
Portsmouth.
Now Home to Home Carpets.
Odeon Theatres Ltd.; 1946 to 1976.
      1936 was proposed to be the Ambassador Cinema. Earlier
      Ambassador Cinema (Cosham Super Cinemas Ltd.); 1937 to
      1940. Presumably replaced the cinema at 29. The new cinema
      was registered by British Projects Ltd., Samuel Berney.
      Originally built as the Ambassador. It became the Odeon in
      1945, seating 1645. Closed in 1976. Now Crown Bingo.
2   Bollom Ltd.; Dyers & Cleaners; 1937 to 1966.
      Later Canton Home Cooked Meats; 1971 to 1976.
1   H & S Ford Ltd.; Boot Repairs; 1948 to 1973.
      Earlier H.S Ford Ltd.; 1937 to 1946.
      Later Allied Shoe Repairs; 1975 to 1976.
1-2   Now Game On, phones, tablets and games.
"My brother remembered the blacksmith's shop behind the Odeon.
Also at the back was the coke tip for the boiler of the Odeon. We went
to Saturday morning pictures when the Yo-Yo championship were on.
I didn't take part as I wasn't particularly good. I liked Woody
Woodpecker, Looney Tunes and serials, there was always a
cliffhanger, and at the start of the next episode it always worked itself
out, also the villain lived to fight another day. Films included the
Dead End Kids, I believe we had some Keystone Kops and lots of
Western Cowboy and Indian films. Dad always took us to the latest
Walt Disney film. The cinema was originally the Ambassador which
was opened by Will Hay in 1937."
      Sylvia Webb

In 1973 a planning application was raised for a new shopping centre, library
etc. which replaces the shops below as far as Havant Road. The library did not
move here.
13a   Smees; Food Stores; 1953 to 1964.
      Earlier Smees; Corn Store; 1928 to 1951.
13a   Thomas Pilcher; Farrier; 1934 to 1967.

13   Fields (Cleaners) Ltd.; Dyers & Cleaners; 1953 to 1964.
11   Smith & Sons (Portsmouth) Ltd.; Bakers. The shopfront was added in 1926.
9   F Arnett; Fishmonger; 1948 to 1967.
Earlier William Drover; Fishmonger; 1934: Mrs Rose Arnett; 1936 to 1946.
7   H.J Weeks; Fried Fish Shop; 1960 to 1962.
Earlier Charles Privett; 1923 to 1946: Mrs C Privett, Fish Fryer; 1948 to 1958.
3   A Latter & Co.; Turf Commission Agents; 1960 to 1964.
Later Jack Grant Ltd.; Turf Commission Agents 1966.
here is Fountain Place (although still shown as a side street the houses were demolished in the 1930s as they were not up to standard.
1   Portsea Island Mutual Co-operative Society Ltd.; Butchers; 1946 to 1964.
Earlier Henry Smith; Butchers; 1918 to 1923: David Brooks; 1928 to 1934: Frank Burt; 1936 to 1940.
here is Havant Road

The new parade of shops replacing 1-13:
As in 2017.
13   Cosham Post Office.
9   Salvation Army Shop.
7   Stan James, Betting Shop.
5   Iceland, Frozen Food & Groceries.
1-3   New Look, Womens' Clothing, Mens Fashion, Teen and Kids Fashion.

The top of the High Street from Spur Road

West Side of High Street
86-124 were added later as a block of flats along the north of the railway line, planning permission being granted in 1956.

84   Lyn Harding; Confectioners; 1960 to 1971.
Earlier William Orford; Confectioners;1946: Thomas Jeffery; Confectioners; 1948 to 1958.
Later R & G (Racing) Ltd.; Turf Accountants; 1973 to 1976.
Now Cosham Independent Barbers.

84a   Cosham Hire Service; Motor Cars for hire; 1960 to 1967.
Later Cosham Taxis 1971: Coast Line Cars; Car Hire; 1973 to 1976.
Now Aquacars, Taxis.

82a   H Ellis; Hairdresser & Cosham Court, Ladies' Hairdresser; 1956 to 1964.
Earlier Elise; Ladies' Hairdresser; 1934: Donald and Ethel McSweeney; Ladies' Hairdresser; 1936 to 1940 (At 87 in 1934): Mrs Ethel McSweeney; 1946: McSweeneys (S.C & V Low); Ladies' Hairdressers; 1948: H Ellis; Hairdresser; 1951 to 1953.
Later T.E Carter; Hairdresser; 1966 to 1976.
Now Vw Taxation Ltd., Tax Consultants

82   Whitehead & Whitehead; Chartered Auctioneers, Estate Agents, Surveyors & Valuers; 1958 to 1964.

82   L Mendel, House Furnisher; 1958 to 1964.
Earlier was Kimbells Ltd.; Restaurant; 1937 to 1940: James Woodhouse & Son; House Furnishers; 1946 to 1956.
Later Mendels; House Furnishers Ltd.; 1966 to 1973. Now Portsmouth Telephones Sports & Social Club.

80 Cinema:
The cinema was built by A.E Porter & Son for The Carlton Cinema Company, planning application 1933. It sat 992 on the ground floor and 302 in the gallery, total 1294.
Carlton Cinema (Associated British Cinemas); 1934 to 1951.
Essoldo Cinema; 1951 to 1971.
Tatler Cinema; 1975.
Classic Cinema; 1976.
Built in 1934 as the Carlton. The cinema was bombed on 5th December 1940. It was restored, opening in December 1941. Complete restoration did not happen until 1949. It closed in 2007 and has since been demolished.

Cosham

"The Essoldo, previously the Carlton Cinema was where we went with Mrs Coates to several films on a Saturday afternoon."
Sylvia Webb.

"It was during the Miner's strike in 1974.The government in their desire to save fuel, instituted a rolling system of power cuts. You could not tell when or where the cuts would take place. The power would be turned off for a few hours in a certain part of the City and then it would be another part of the city's turn.
A group of us used to regularly go to the cinema usually on a Tuesday evening. This particular evening we went to see a film at the ABC cinema in Commercial Road. Halfway through the film the power went off in that area of the city so we had only seen half of the film. One of our group knew that the same film was being shown at the Essoldo cinema in Cosham. So we left the ABC cinema in Commercial Road and got into our cars and went to Cosham. We were under the impression that they were both belonging to the same chain. We entered the Essoldo Cosham and told the receptionist about the loss of power at the ABC and the fact that we had only seen half the film. She allowed us in (for free) and we saw the rest of the film. It was only later in the evening that we realised that the two cinemas were not in the same organisation."
Peter Galvin

"Mum is only four foot eleven inches tall and she drove a Wessex Terraplane ambulance for the ARP post at Futchers School. It was navy blue with a red cross and was kept in use up to the 1950s. I remember her pointing it out to me as a child, when the ambulances were parked at the gateway to St Mary's Hospital. She said they put wooden blocks on the pedals so she could reach them. One day my nan, her mother, said she was going to the Carlton Cinema in Cosham, with my grandad to see Elizabeth and Essex starring Errol Flynn. That afternoon the cinema was bombed and she was sent with my auntie to pick up casualties in her ambulance. She was picking up people with their arms blown off and ferrying them to St Mary's, all the time looking for her parents. She got home dirty and tired at 6pm and found my Nan in a fury scrubbing the kitchen floor. Grandad had to work that afternoon and let her down so she missed the film, but she didn't know the bomb had hit the cinema. It seems amazing today that there

were no mobiles or any other way of contacting her parents. She was relieved to find her mum at home safe."
Jean Ridgeon

The site of the cinema is now Harding House, 35 flats, on the High Street frontage with Ockendon House, 23 flats, at the rear built by PMC Construction & Development Services Ltd. for First Wessex. The architect was Kenn Scadden Associates Ltd., built in 2016. PMC have offices on the ground floor.

78   Palm Court Restaurant; 1956 to 1971.
      "An open front style coffee bar. Large potted palms or ferns inside. Often used by the local teddy boys in the evenings."
      Malcolm Garlick

      Earlier A Hassell; Snack Bar; 1951: Cosham Cafés Ltd.; Café; 1953. A planning application was raised for Meon House, 14 flats at 78 with Meon Mews, 8 flats at the rear accessed from Vectis Way in 2005. The ground floor of Meon House has two shops:
      78a R & B Pets Pantry
      78b Funky Baby Boutique

76   Finlay & Co. Ltd.; Tobacconists; 1960 to 1966.
      Earlier Albert Butcher & Co.; 1934: A Butcher; Tobacconist; 1936 to 1938: Harvey's; Tobacconist; 1940 to 1958.
74   Smith & Vosper Ltd.; Bakers; 1934 to 1971.
72   Electricity Show Rooms:
      Portsmouth Electric Light; 1934.
      City of Portsmouth Electricity Undertaking; 1936 to 1946. The showrooms were damaged by a bomb in 1941.
      Southern Electricity Board, 1948 to 1976.
72-76 a planning application was raised for rebuilding as shops and flats in 2003 with Bosun Court on High Street frontage and Capstan House at rear; and Quarterdeck, 11 flats in Vectis Way, architects PLC Architects. Bosun Court has shops on the ground floor:
      74   Dolphin Orthodontics.
      72   Total Look, Hairdressers.

70   Whitmore Jones Ltd.; House Furnishers; 1936 to 1976.
      Earlier Whitmore Jones; 1934.

The shop was built in 1928 and they finally closed in 1981.
Now Finishing Touch, Carpets & Vinyl.
68   Geoffrey Cole; Chemist;1951 to 1966.
Later G.M Guernier; 1967 to 1976.
Everett; Chemist 1994.
Now Home Coffee Cosham, also at Albert Road, Southsea.
66-64 Central Buildings built in 1930, see plaque in the parapet
66   K Rodaway; Butcher; 1960 to 1976.
Earlier C.H Cotton Ltd.; Butchers; 1936 to 1956.
Now Prime Lettings & PMBS (Project Managed Building Services, founded in 2013).
64   John Mason; Boot Maker; 1946 to 1971.
Earlier George Westaway; Boot Repairs; 1934 to 1940.
Later John Mason (Footwear) Ltd.; 1973 to 1976.
In 2010 a planning application was raised for change of use to a restaurant. Now Palace Café Restaurant.
62   Portsmouth Trading Co. Ltd.; Builders' Merchants; 1938 to 1960.
Earlier A.E Porter & Sons Ltd.; Builders' Merchants; 1934 to 1936.
Later Baileys Do-It-Yourself-Supplies; 1966 to 1967: Forton Supplies; Do It Yourself; 1971.
In 1974 a planning application was raised for the building of a banking hall and two flats, Barclays Bank. The bank premises on the ground floor are now empty.
A new one way system means cars going north have to turn down Vectis Way.
here is Vectis Way
The Priory, High Street;
1881 to 1904; Matthew Hudson, Missionary
The Priory; Hudson Brothers; Cabinet Makers & Home of Rest for Christians; 1901 to 1905. The Priory, High Street; 1911 to 1914; Matthew Hudson, Missionary.
The Priory, 58 High Street; 1917 to 1918; Matthew Hudson; Missionary.
In 1936 Portsmouth & Gosport Gas Company applied for permission to build on the site of St Faith's Mission, at 58 High Street.
Note the date in the pediment when the premises were built 1937.
Portsmouth & Gosport Gas Company; Showrooms; 1940 to 1948.
Portsmouth, Gosport & Bognor Regis Gas Undertaking; Showrooms; 1951 to 1956.
Southern Gas Board (Wight & Portsmouth); Showrooms; 1958 to 1976.

Cosham

"The gas showrooms were where Pamela Boothby and myself went to monthly meetings of Young Homemakers, mostly swapping recipes and other hints on running a home."
Sylvia Webb

Later in 1995 a planning application was raised for 58-60 for Everett Pharmacy which is still there.

A planning application was raised for new shops & offices alongside in 1957.
58d   Are offices above the ground floor shops. Liverpool Victoria Friendly Society; 1962 to 1967. Now Relate.
58c   Bendix Launderette; 1960 to 1964.
Later Frigidaire Washerteria 1966 to 1976.
Now Dixies Bar.
58b   Mrs D Merrick; Wool Stores. 1962 to 1971.
In 2001 a planning application was raised for change of use for hot food and drink on the premises and take away. Now King Chef, Chinese takeaway.
58a   Muriel Roberts; Ladies' Fashions.
Now AJM Estate Agents.
50-56 were rebuilt as 5 shops planning application in 1966.
     56   Liverpool Victoria Friendly Society, 1960.
     56c   Above the shops, now Ultrasound Direct - Baby Bond.
     56b   Adams (Carpets) Ltd.; 1971 to 1976.
         Book Stack Books in 1994.
         New to You, Book Shop; 2013 to 2017.
     56a   Kwongon; Chinese Restaurant; 1971 to 1976.
         Now Cosham Kebab House.
54   A.S Ashley; House Furnisher. Ashleys 1962 to 1966.
Smith & Vosper Ltd.; Bakers; 1973 to 1976.
Later Boo Boo Sandwich Bar, Opened by sisters Caroline Nash & Sarah Hussey in May 2014. Now Kare Plus, Care Agency.
52   J Greenhouse; Photographer; 1960 to 1966. Earlier listed at 54; 1953 to 1958.
"He did the traditional family portraits and wedding photos."

Earlier John Sutton-Jarvis; Chemist; 1934 to 1940.
Later Halfords Ltd.; Motor Car Accessories; 1973 to 1976.
Now Lloyds Pharmacy.
52a   Verena Wool Shop (V & R.E Rourke, 1958); 1958 to 1964.

Earlier Mrs L.M Bevis; Wool Stores; 1956.

50   Brunswick Dyeing & Cleaning Co. Ltd. & Brunswick Family Laundry Co. Ltd.; 1958 to 1967. Earlier they were at 105; 1934 to 1956.
Now Bet Fred.

50a   Peter Graham (Portsmouth) Ltd.; Fabric Dealers; 1960 to 1962.
"Later from around 1961 was Sheila's Baby Carriages run by a family by the name of Forbes."
Malcolm Garlick

50b   J.H Watson; Dental Surgeon. M Pike; Dental Surgeon; 1967 to 1971.

"The road widened here until it reached the Ship, public house. There was an area of open land stretching to the Northern Road, edged with a high fence. It contained what looked like a bandstand."
Malcolm Garlick

"I remember the Ship Inn. I believe there was a bus stop and hoarding outside. They built a supermarket and café and the 1st floor in the space that was vacant."
Frank Thompson

The numbering around 48 is confusing as part of the site was vacant and the site has been split up, without the street being renumbered.

48a-f   In 1959 a planning application was raised for supermarket, shop and flats, Pearl Assurance House, 48d-48b
    48f   Fine Fare Supermarkets Ltd. 1964 to 1976.
           Peacocks since at least 1994.
    48d   Corbins Footwear Ltd.; 1964 to 1976.
    48e   Harveys Card Specialists; 1971: Tees Card Centre; 1973 to 1976.
           Now Naomi House; Charity Shop.
    48d   Barries; Ladies' Outfitter; 1971.
           Now Dominos Pizza.
    48   Now Flutes Café.
    48b   Now empty.

Cosham

An early postcard view of the Ship showing how it laid at an angle

48   Listed as The Ship Inn or Ship from 1830 to 1958 in the trade directories. Despite the new shops being listed the pub is still listed up until 1976 in the directories - did it survive as a smaller pub in the modern rebuild or are the directories in error?

An early 1900s view shows this as a large building with two projecting gabled ends with a verandah at the front. It was set back from the road.

"The Ship was where I went with my friend Barbara and her parents, Mr & Mrs Calder, when at aged 16 we were on our way to a Co-op Ball at South Parade Pier. We were allowed beer shandy or Babycham. Stories we heard were of men having fights and often being thrown out of the window, certainly Cosham had a reputation of being rough in those days."
    Sylvia Webb

"Sometimes could be quite rough and some of the happenings could not be printed!"
    Malcolm Garlick

48d-48 A pair of properties with:
48d   Boots, Pharmacy & Beauty
48   W.H Smith, Booksellers

42-46   A planning application was raised in 1962 to rebuild, 42 was split into two 1983, 42a pub 1997.

46   G & G Curtis Ltd.; Seed Merchants, Grocers & Haulage Contractors; 1897 to 1960.
Was a three storey building with doors on each floor served by a hoist projecting from the eaves.
"The entrance was up two steps from the pavement. There were sacks of seed all around. I recall a centre support column."
      Malcolm Garlick
"Animal feed store, a real old fashioned store."
      Arthur Collins

The premises were rebuilt
- 46   Bakers of Cosham (Baker & Son (Chemists) Ltd.); 1966 to 1973. See number 42.
Later Trustee Savings Bank, 1975 to 1976.
- 46a   Now Specsavers.
- 46   Now Poppins Café. The Poppins Restaurateurs Association was formed in 1979, all the 36 restaurants are independently owned but operate the same model.

44   Baker & Son; Booksellers & Stationers; 1958 to 1962.
May earlier have been Park View Villa
Earlier Cosham Book Shop; 1953 to 1956.
Later
- 44b   Solent Cleaners 1966 to 1976.
      Now Solent Dry Cleaners.
- 44a Westminster Bank Ltd. 1966 to 1973.
      Now British Heart Foundation, Charity Shop

42   Chemist:
Established in 1845 by Thomas Brown Baker in premises on the east side of the High Street. He died in 1901 and his nephew, Cyril Baker, son of his younger brother, Alfred Philip Baker, became the owner. Returning from London where his father was a pharmacist. The business was made a private company in 1948, Baker & Son (Chemists) Ltd. In 1957 the business was bought by the manager, Mr J.P Barlow who retained the name. The business moved to number 46 when the street was widened. The business closed on 2nd June 1973 at 46 High Street.
Directories and census show the following:
Directories Thomas Baker; Chemist;1847 to 1885.

Cosham

1851 Census Thomas Brown Baker, 24, Chemist & Druggist, next to Swan.
1861 Census Thomas Brown Baker, 34, Chemist & Druggist, sons George, 10; Thomas, 9; next to Swan.
1871 Census Thomas Brown Baker, 44, Post Office, Chemist & Druggist, sons Alfred J, 9; Arthur E, 7; William H, 5; next to Swan
1881 Census Thomas Brown Baker, 53, Post Office & Pharmacy, sons Alfred J, 19, Dentist; Arthur E, 17, Dentist; William H, 15; next to Swan
Directories Thomas Baker & Son; Chemist; 1886 to 1889.
1891 Census Thomas Brown Baker, 64, Dental Surgeon & Chemist, sons William Herbert, 25, Chemist; next to Swan.
Directories
1901 census; Cyril Baker, 24, Chemist in High Street, next to Swan.
Baker & Son; Chemist; 42; 1905 to 1920.
Baker & Son; Chemists; 42-44; 1923 to 1937.
Baker & Son (Chemists) Ltd.; 42-44; 1938 to 1951.
Baker & Son (Chemists) Ltd.; 1953 to 1964.
"The shop was double fronted and in each window was a large carbuoy, one red, one blue. They probably seemed a lot bigger than they really were but when you were little everything seemed larger."
Malcolm Garlick
"They has large glass containers with coloured liquid in!
Arthur Collins

The shop was rebuilt in 1966 as a terrace of four shops.
Victor Value & Co. Ltd.; Grocers; 1966 to 1967. Tesco; Supermarket; 1971 to 1976.
42a   The First Post, a J.D Weatherspoons Pub, opened 8th December 1988. Stands on the site of shop built in 1840s.
42b   Now Ladbrokes, Betting Shop
40   Listed in the trade directories from 1830 as Swan, Swan Hotel or Swan Inn. In 2016 the Swan, Punch Taverns. It was rebuilt for Brickwoods in 1935. It closed in 2016, the interior gutted and work continues on the building with 4 retail units and 5 flats being formed including a three storey extension at the rear.
"There was always a sing song on a Saturday night"
Sylvia Webb

here is Wayte Street

38a	George Lock; Greengrocer/Fruiterer; 1934 to 1964.

38a George Lock; Greengrocer/Fruiterer; 1934 to 1964.
Later Wiltons; Fruiterers 1966 to 1976.
Now The Sandwich Shop.

38 J.H Dewhurst Ltd.; Butchers; 1936 to 1976.
In 2007 a planning application was made for change of use to café/restaurant.
Now Ninos Café since 2011.

34-36 Timothy Whites; Chemists; 1953 to 1967.
Earlier Timothy Whites Ltd.; 1928 to 1934: Timothy Whites & Taylors Ltd.; 1936 to 1951.
Later Boots The Chemist; 1971 to 1976.
Now M & Co., Womens & Mens Clothing.

32 F.G Currey Ltd.; Pork Butchers; 1934 to 1971. Shopfront 1931 for Mr Currey.
Now H&T Pawnbrokers.

30 Finlay & Co. Ltd.; Tobacconists; 1960 to 1976.
Earlier Harvey's; Tobacconists; 1940 to 1958.
The shopfront was added in 1929 for Miss A Couzens.
Was until recently a branch of Large & Large, Opticians. Established by Rupert & Trudy Large the original shop remains at Waterlooville.

30a Walter Dear; Chiropodist; 1951 to 1967.
"I went to him after an unsuccessful hospital treatment fo a toe that had grown septic due to an ingrown toenail. A brilliant result from him!"
Malcolm Garlick

28 Barclays Bank Ltd.; 1934 to 1976.
Earlier Elizabeth Pettingell; Harness Maker & Sadler; 1881 to 1918.
Now Nationwide, Building Society.

26 Westons; Bakers; 1958 to 1962.
Later F Wilkins (1930) Ltd.; Bakers; 1964 to 1976.
In 2005 planning application was raised for the Card Factory which is still trading here.

24 Zip French Cleaners Ltd.; Dyers & Cleaners; 1953 to 1964.
Earlier E.W Honess & Sons; Dyers & Cleaners; 1934 to 1951.
Was an Oxfam, Charity Shop 1973 to 2014, now Headway - Brain Injury, Charity Shop.

22 Pearks Dairies Ltd.; Grocers; 1953 to 1962.
Now Cry, Charity Shop.

20 Osbornes Stores Ltd.; Grocers; 1934 to 1960.

Cosham

Now Penelope's Petals, Florist.
18   Campions (Bakers) Ltd.; 1934 to 1973.
Now Greggs, Bakers.
16   National Provincial Bank Ltd.; 1921 to 1971. In 1931 the bank was
rebuilt by A.E Porter & Son.
Later National Westminster Bank Ltd.; 1973.
Earlier was The Falcon; 1847 to 1920. The pub closed and was sold
in the 1920s. The Falcon from the pediment was moved to number 14
when the pub was demolished and the bank built on the site.
Now Lloyds Bank.

City of Portsmouth Building School; Annexe; 1953 to 1960.
This was earlier the National School, built in 1849 at a cost of £500.
It was enlarged in 1866, at a cost £170. This was built on the site of
another pub, The Anchor.
1852; Master Benjamin Caeser, Mistress Matilda Caeser.
1875 to 1878; Master Benjamin Caeser, Infants Miss Ellen Warwick
Later it became the Elementary School for Boys 1936 to 1951; Girls;
1928 to 1934, Girls & Boys; 1923.
"We always thought the building was an old church as it was built in
flint. In the 1950s there were two main areas for teaching metalwork
and woodwork."
Malcolm Garlick

"The Building School was where my husband, David Webb, went and
nearby Ye Olde Sweete Shop which we visited before going to the
Saturday morning pictures at the Odeon opposite."
Sylvia Webb

Now Tesco, Metro Store.

14   L.T Cole & Sons (Portsmouth) Ltd.; Confectioners; 1960.
Earlier Smith Eden Ltd.; Tobacconists/Confectioners; 1914 to 1948:
F.H.O Duckworth; Confectioners; 1951 to 1958.
Later J.L Cole 1962 to 1976. In September 1973 a planning
application was raised for consent to demolish a listed building. In
1982 described in Hampshire Treasures as 18th Century facade to an
earlier building. Two shallow bow windows on ground floor.
Now Barnados, Charity Shop.

Numbers 10-12 first had shopfront added in 1935 by S Berney, builder of Portsmouth.

12   Portsmouth & Sunderland Newspapers Ltd.; 1948 to 1967.

10   E.W Cracknell & Son; Outfitters; 1946 to 1967.

10-12 are now the Halifax Bank.

Asherfield Buildings; 1934 to 1976.

Was earlier Asherfield House, a Victorian villa.

George Hall King, Solicitor; 1885 to 1888.

John Walter Boughton, manager of the Theatre Royal; 1889 to 1914.

A Clark Mills; 1917 to 1918.

8 High Street, A Clarke Mills; 1923.

8 Olaf Glees on; Physician & Surgeon; 1928.

It was bought from the Doctor by Bert Clifton and partner Arthur Abbs. The ground floor was converted into a shop in 1930. The house was destroyed by fire on 12th April 1984. Asher field Buildings were built on the site.

8   Decorators' & Builders' Merchants:
Asherfield Ltd.; Decorators' Merchants; 1956 to 1960.
Earlier Clifton & Mabbs; House Decorators at 6; 1928: Clifton & Mabbs; House Decorators; 1934: Herbert Clifton; Builders' Merchant; 1936 to 1938: Barnes & Son Ltd.; Builders' & Decorators' Merchants; 1940: Asherfield Ltd. (Formerly Barnes & Son Ltd.); 1946 to 1953.
Later Barnes & Son Ltd.; Decorators' Merchants; 1962 to 1971: Barnes (PGW Holdings Ltd.); Decorators' Merchants; 1973 to 1976.
Now PamPurred Pets.

8b   Now Good Deal.

earlier between 8 and 6 was Budds Place; 1923 to 1928.

6   David Greig Ltd.; 1962 to 1976.
"Who sold the best ham, carved while you wait."
     Arthur Collins

Now Hair OTT, established in 1976, with branches in North End and later Waterlooville, Lakeside and Whiteley.

4   Smith & Vosper Ltd.; Grocers; 1956 to 1960. Earlier at 6; 1936 to 1953.
Now Cosham Decor.

Cosham

2   O.P Lighting. Closed in 2014 after 42 years. Run by John
     Horne. Shop since absorbed by Cosham Decor.
here are Spur & London Roads

London Road

The old houses either side of the road have been demolished and new flats
built. At some dates the road is referred to as High Street, which it is a
continuation of.

West Side of London Road
Red Lion Hotel:

In 1927 discussions were held between Portsmouth Council and Henty
& Constable re the land at the junction of High Street and the
proposed Spur Road. Part of the land acquired from Mr Stubbs is now
not required to be conveyed to Henty & Constable who shall apply for
the closing of Church Path also they would convey part of the land
fronting London Road to the council to facilitate the widening of
London Road. When rebuilt the new public house should be set back
16 feet from Spur Road. In 1928 there were two planning applications
by Henty & Constable for the rebuilding.

Anida Rayfield in the book Discovering Cosham states that the Red
Lion was first listed in 1712 with Mr Penford, and rebuilt in 1932 after
discussions begun in 1926 due to the building of Spur Road.
In the trade directories the pub is listed from 1839 as Red Lion or Red
Lion Hotel and is still there today as the Red Lion Hotel.
The pub had a major renovation in February 2014 and has recently
been bought by Mitchells & Butlers from the Orchid Group.

The old milestone still stands on the pavement at the rear of the Red Lion. The
east facing side has been fitted with a new plaque with the milages. The west
face has some faint traces of lettering with different milage as the road has
been straightened/realigned .

19   B Roberts; Greengrocer; 1958 to 1967.
At the rear of the pub up to the hill road were some old cottages.
Chalk Cottage; 1739 to 1970; London Road, near the Red Lion. Built of chalk
with cement render added later. Demolished 1970.

Milestone Cottages, also known as Flint Cottages 1-2; 1750 to 1970; London Road, near Red Lion. Also demolished 1970. Named after the Portsmouth-London Milestone in London Road. The site of all these cottages is now a car park.

East Side of London Road
On the 1879 map there is a large house, on the corner of London Road/Havant Road opposite the Red Lion, called Knapps House. In the 1881 census there is a Knapps Terrace, 1-12, in Havant Road to Knapp House which was occupied by Thomas Canning a brewer employing 6 men.
here is the entrance to Widley Street

Portsdown House
    Anida Rayfield in the book Discovering Cosham states that the pediment over the door had the initials CA
    Capt later Major George Aylward; Lime Merchant;1886 to 1918. In 1881 he was at 1 Widley Terrace, Lime Merchant, employing 5 men. He retired on 30th June 1939. So the initials should probably be GA.
    In 1939 the owner H.T Clifton was prepared to let the ground floor and one upstairs room to be used as a Ward Centre for the Air defence Committee for ARP use.
    Collis & Co. (Tobacco) Ltd.; 1946 to 1960.
    City of Portsmouth Public Health Dept, Citizens' Advice Bureau; 1971 to 1973.
        "When I started as a clerk in the Public Health Dept. in 1964, I was told I was to cover the 2 weeks leave of the clerk at this north Portsmouth office. On the ground floor were four Public Health Inspectors and upstairs were a number of Health Visitors. I had to take care of the switchboard, do a bit of typing and deal with any queries. I think the office closed late in the 60s."
        Alan Eamey

58 Wansley, Cyril Woodman; Dentist; 1937 to 1960.
here is Widley Road

Cosham

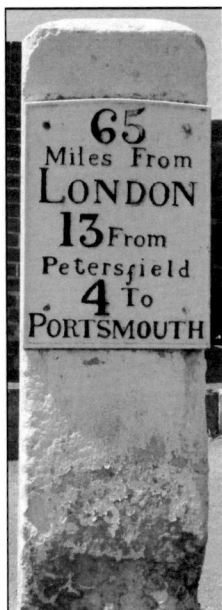

65
Miles From
LONDON
13 From
Petersfield
4 To
PORTSMOUTH

Chalk Cottage

Flint Cottages

Cosham

An old view for the road looking north with Portsdown House behind the cottage

Cosham

Another old view looking south

Northern Road
Only the east side from the railway north will be covered as the west side is
Wymering in our earlier booklet on Wymering and Paulsgrove.
The Great North Road as it was called in planning documents in 1922 had
been thought about for many years previously. It was only in 1920 when
Cosham became part of Portsmouth that the discussions became more
serious. It was to be a hundred foot wide highway from the Green Posts at
Hilsea to the Havant Road, then an eighty foot wide highway to the top of
the hill. The early plans included widening of the High Street, rather than
the solution which was adopted with a new road to the west. The new road
was opened on 28th May 1925.

Portsmouth Trunk Telephone Exchange was built in 1973 and later
extended. Earlier the old telephone exchange was part of the Post Office
buildings on the other side of the road.
here is footpath to Vectis Way
Later Cosham Community Centre and the Health Centre were here.
here is Wayte Street

52 Beresford	Edward O Day; Dental Surgeon; 1956 to 1958.
	E.O Day & R.J Gutteridge; Dental Surgeons; 1960 to 1962.
	E.O Day, R.J Gutteridge & E.B Bonar; Dental Surgeons; 1964.
	E.O Day & R.J Gutteridge; Dental Surgeons; 1966 to 1973. Now the offices for Hampshire Genealogical Society who have been here since 2012. See their website www.hgs-familyhistory.com.
52a	At the rear is Cartek Garage Services, Daniel Goddard & Damien Shawyer, established in 2012.
54	Now ARC, Drug & Alcohol Rehab Centre.
56 Rosgar	John Norman Sampson& R Reddy; Physicians & Surgeons; 1956 to 1958. John Norman Sampson & R Reddy; Physicians & Surgeons; 1960. John Norman Sampson, R Reddy, John Mainwaring; 1962. R.D Reddy & John Mainwaring; Physicians & Surgeons; 1964 to 1966. K Rich & John Mainwaring; Physicians & Surgeons; 1967. K Rich, John Mainwaring & J Sheehan; Physicians &

Surgeons; 1971 to 1976.
Now Northern Road Surgery.
58 Stokes, Neville-Smith & Grubb; Solicitors; 1960 to 1976.
Now Kingfisher Property Group Ltd., incorporated in 2016.
60 Thrums Kenneth Woolas; Physician & Surgeon; 1956 to 1960.
Kenneth Woolas & Peter Cameron; Physicians & Surgeons; 1962 to 1976.
60-62 are now Churchers, Solicitors.
64 Now Zen Beauty Spa and Chiropody & Podiatry Centre.
here is Spur Road
90 Highcliffe J Blatt; Dental Surgeon; 1958.
J & Mrs Blatt; Dental Surgeons; 1960 to 1962.
J & Mrs Blatt & Charles Sutterby; Dental Surgeons; 1964 to 1976.

Spur Road
This road is mentioned in the town planning committees as a new proposed by-pass road in 1926, to be built partly on Mr Stubbs' garage. Earlier Church Path led from the High street to Wymering on a slightly different alignment.
In 1928 a planning application was raised for 4 houses, a bungalow, then 4 more houses.
The roundabout at the junction with Northern Road used to be known as the Compass Roundabout as the approach roads instead the of current practice of just arrows used to be painted with N,E,W,S in the lanes.

North Side of Spur Road
Red Lion, see High Street.
City of Portsmouth Public Libraries, Cosham Branch; 1936 to 1975.
Hampshire County Libraries; 1976. Now back to Portsmouth Libraries.
Earlier the library was in part of Cosham Picture House, in 1926 to 1927. The new library was built by Cortis & Hankins Ltd. of Farlington for £2979.
2 Now The Natural Therapy Centre.
4 Now AMR Bookkeepers & Accounts.
8 Goodman & Kent; Solicitors; 1960 to 1967.
Warner Goodman & Co.; Solicitors; 1971 to 1976.

10   Now KSL Accountants & Business Advisors.

South Side of Spur Road
1   Chocolate Box; Confectioners; 1958 to 1962.
        Later Maynards Ltd.; Confectioners; 1964 to 1976.
3   Cooper & Sons; Butchers; 1958 to 1967.
        Now Tasty Plaice, Fish & Chip Shop.
3A   Suitalls; Outfitters; 1958 to 1976.
        Now Vision Travel.
5   Now Bargain Booze.
7   Clifford Leal; Florist; 1946 to 1964.
        Later A.C Leal & Co. Ltd.; Florists; were at 21; 1967 to 1976.
        Now A Matter of Taste; Kebab Shop.
9 (Houghton)   S.F Doran; Dental Surgeon; 1946 to 1967.
        "There was a dentist at 9 Spur Road. I was taken there in the mid
        1940s for toothache, aged about 5. Treatment was just to dab some
        whiskey on the affected tooth and nothing else. I can't remember if
        it worked!"
                Malcolm Garlick

        9-11 Now Cosham Conservative Club.
11   Milly's Restaurant & Café (Mrs G.W Graham); 1948 to 1960.
        Earlier John Worrall; Café; 1938 to 1940: William Carter; Café;
        1946.
        Later Mrs G.W Graham; Café; 1962 to 1975.
13   Art Needlework Stores (Mrs E Curtis); 1946 to 1960.
        Now Cosham Osteopathic Clinic.
15   Clifford Leal; Greengrocer; 1940 to 1964.
        Now Rainbow Chinese Take Away.
17   Alfred Tree; Hairdresser; 1946 to 1964.
        Later R.A Cleeve; Hairdresser; 1966 to 1976.
        Now Ian Henry; Hairdresser for Men, established in 1928.
19   Dashwood & Denyer Ltd.; Funeral Directors; 1940 to 1976.
        Earlier William H Dashwood; Undertaker; 1936 to 1938.
        Now the Grill Out, Peri-Peri, Burgers etc.
21   William Lambert & Son; Shopkeepers; 1956 to 1964.
        Earlier William Lambert; Shopkeeper; 1940 to 1953.
        Now U-Name-It
23-25   Young & White; Auctioneers; 1956 to 1976.
        Now Hill House; Copy That; Printing, Copying Video etc

25   Portsmouth Trustee Savings Bank; 1958 to 1973.

Clock House   Hall, Pain & Foster; Estate Agents; 1956 to 1967.
Now the Discount Window Centre.

Vectis Way
North Side of Vectis Way
Cosham Civic Centre; 1945 to 1971.
The building was earlier Cosham & District Services Club, built in
1940 to provide facilities for the large number of servicemen in the
area. Sold to the city council for £2,560 in 1945.
St Peter's & St Paul's Church Hall; 1960 to 1967.
Now Cosham Health Centre, Cosham Dental Centre and Cosham
Community Centre

South Side of Vectis Way
Royal Air Force Association (Cosham Branch); 1956 to 1967.

Wayte Street
This was formerly the start of Southampton Road, until 1958, which carried
on along what is now Medina Road. The new Southampton Road was cut
through to the north later.

North Side of Wayte Street
2-12 all the same style, single storey shops.
2   Littlemodes; Childrens' Outfitter; 1960 to 1976.
Earlier George Lock; Fruiterer & Greengrocer; 1946: J Dagastino
(Portsmouth) Ltd.; Ice Cream Merchants; 1948 to 1958.
Now Sweeney Todd; Barbers.
4   G.W Green Ltd.; Bakers; 1956 to 1975.
Earlier Kimbells Ltd.; Bakers; 1946 to 1953.
6   1960; Not Listed.
Stock & Lunt; Physicians & Surgeons; 1962 to 1971.
4-6 Now empty.
8   Ganly; Grocers; 1956 to 1976.
Now Pretty Pretty Nails.
10   Linden Enterprises (Portsmouth) Ltd.; Hire Purchase Finance
House; 1956 to 1960.

Cosham

Later 10-12; Jim's; House Furnishers; 1962.
10; Braiden & Thomas Ltd.; Photographic & Cine Specialists;
1964 to 1971.
Cosham Cameras Ltd.; 1973 to 1976.
Now Top Dog Tattoos.

12 Hobson, Sherwell & Wells; Solicitors; 1946 to 1960.
Later R Ingram; Shop; 1964;
A & B Bazaars; 1966 to 1967;
Harvey's; Fancy Goods; 1971 to 1976.
Now Alice Lou; Wool Shop.

14 Portsmouth Trade Union Club & Institute Ltd.; 1946 to 1976.
Now Cosham Social Club
Earlier was number 4; 1934 to 1940. Built in 1932 as can been seen
on the plaque on the front.

18-23 all the same style, single storey shops.

18 Haywards; Handicraft Supplies; 1960 to 1967.
Later Hayward's; Model Dealers; 1971 to 1976. Later Haywards;
Second Hand Shop.
Now Baby Shop.

20 L.T Cole & Sons (Portsmouth) Ltd.; Confectioners; 1960 to 1971.
Later C.F Marshall; Confectioners; 1973 to 1976.
Later Cosham Newsagents.
Now Gandhi Indian Takeaway.

22 Colortone; Decorators' Merchants; 1960 to 1976.
Now Marjories Tearoom & Bistro.

24 G.J & J.W Wilkins; Ladies' Hairdresser; 1960 to 1967.
Later Eileen's Hair Fashions; 1971 to 1976.
Later The Cutting Company.
Now Alekandser Budis; Hair Studio.

Mrs Honor Wayte; Almshouses listed here 1940.
In 1600 Honor Wayte (or Waite), by deed, granted to trustees her
interest in a lease for 5,000 years acquired by her in 1594 of a
messuage, orchard and garden in Cosham, upon which she had settled
a poor house for four poor, honest women, and a yearly rent of 6s 8d
to be paid out of a garden in Cosham called Stakes Garden, and a
yearly rent of £6 to be paid out of the Manor of Denmead to the intent
that the said messuage and premises should for ever remain a dwelling
house for four poor sole women of Wymering, or failing such out of
the parish of Wickham; the said yearly rent of 6s 8d to be employed

Cosham

about repairing of the said house, and such uses as the charity as the trustees should think most meet, and the said annuity of £6 to be divided equally among the four occupants. The rent of 6s 8d is duly paid by Thomas Thistlethwayte, and the annuity paid by Mr John Kennett and equally divided among the four occupants, who also receive the benefit in fuel of the interest of £100 consols bequeathed in 1818 by the will of John Soaper and of £100 consols given in 1839 by the Rev James Henville (Vicar of Wymering). The income of another sum of £100 consols belonging to the charity of the Rev John Taylor is also received by the occupants. Rev John Taylor, Rector of Widley and Vicar of Wymering by deed gave £100 consols for the benefit of the two said parishes, and declared that out of the annual income £2 should be applied in purchasing Bibles, Prayer Books, and other pious books, to be distributed amongst the poor of the two parishes. When that end had been fully answered, the £2 should be applied in instructing poor children of the two parishes to read and write, and the residue of the income towards repairing the almshouses at Wymering founded by Honor Wayte. The income of the charity has for some years, at the discretion of the trustees, been applied for the benefit of the Cosham Almshouses.

Victoria County History, 1908.

The original almshouse consisted of a small thatched building containing two rooms above and two below, situated in a garden of less then ½ an acre. In1817 it was accidentally burnt down and rebuilt by subscription. It now consists of four rooms on the ground floor inhabited by 4 poor women of the parish.

Charity Commissioners 1837

The rebuilt Almshouses were a terrace with a plaque in the pediment.

In 1594 the house, orchard and garden where four women lived was granted to Honor Wayte by William Crossweller of Harting, West Sussex, for the term of 5,000 years. The charity sold the almshouses in 1957. The Charity Commisioners suggested that the Honor Wayte, John Soaper, Charles Brune Henville and William Herbert Baker charities be merged under the new Honor Waite Charity.

The News

The charity was still in existence in 2012 as the Honor Waite Relief in Need Charity, registered in 1965, No 239465, making grants to needy elderly single women or widows in Wymering. The accounts have not been filed for since 2012.

The above picture from Gates Illustrated History shows the Almshouses

Portsmouth Corporation (Yard); 1940 to 1976. Now the entrance to the Tesco car park.
Portsmouth City Fire Brigade, Station 3; 1953 to 1973.
> A planning application was submitted in 1950 for a new fire station. The tender of V.H Dye for £18,892 16s 3d was accepted. On 1st Jan 1952 the new station was opened by the Lord Mayor, the first new permanent station opened after the war.
> Later Hampshire Fire Brigade, Station 3; 1975 to 1976.

> "The wartime British Restaurant was on the site that is now the fire station."
> Arthur Collins

South Side of Wayte Street

1-5   Part of the Swan public house, see High Street.

here is Wootton Street

7-11   Marriots (Cosham) Ltd.; House Furnishers; 1960 to 1967. Planning application for showroom, extended 1959.
1969 planning application for use of showroom for sale of motor cars. Dove & Son; Used Cars; 1971. J Dove & Son, Motor Car Agents; 1973 to 1976.
Now Peelers Gate flats, planning application for 34 flats 2002.

In 1942 the land was bought for £7,000 for new Police Station. The tender of J.H Day for £49,030 was accepted.
Portsmouth City Police; D Division; 1956 to 1967. Earlier Portsmouth City Police; 1953. Later Hampshire Constabulary (Havant Division) (Cosham Sub-Division); 1971 to 1976.
Still a Police Station.